HODDER HOME LEARNING

English f brighter child

AGE 7-9

Rhona Whiteford and Jim Fitzsimmons

Illustrated by Chantal Kees

This workbook has been designed for the child who has a good grasp of English.

The book provides activities which span the **Reading** and **Writing** elements of the English curriculum. The activities become progressively more difficult. Six tests are included to give a record of progress.

How to help your child

- Keep sessions short and regular.
- The exercises are intended to be enjoyable as well as educational so always stop if your child is not relaxed or has lost concentration.
- Build confidence. Offer plenty of praise and encouragement.
- Use practical opportunities for reading and writing in daily life.
- Encourage accurate spelling, clear handwriting and imaginative use of language.

Hodder Children's Books

NATIONAL CONFEDERATION OF PARENT TEACHER ASSOCIATIONS

The only home learning programme supported by the NCPTA

Hidden words

WRITING: SPELLING

1 – 10 **oi** and **oy** can make the same sound.

join **joy**

Find the **oi** words. Colour them red.

p	l	o	r	o	y	a	l	i	t
c	a	n	s	r	o	i	l	k	p
p	r	p	o	i	n	t	o	s	k
d	o	l	o	y	s	t	e	r	n
a	m	t	o	x	l	e	b	o	y
b	a	n	n	o	y	x	o	z	y
o	i	j	a	s	o	i	l	r	i
v	r	f	o	i	l	t	o	o	l
m	p	r	k	b	o	i	l	o	o
i	o	s	e	n	j	o	y	b	e

Find the **oy** words. Colour them green.

Choose an **oi** word or an **oy** word to answer each clue.

11 **To show someone the way** p

12 **A prince is a member of a** r **family.**

13 **Silver paper** f

14 **A child who is not a girl is a** b **.**

15 **To make water very hot** b

16 **A shellfish** o

17 **If you have a good time you** e **yourself.**

18 **Plants grow in this.** s

Now write the eight words in alphabetical order.

19 20 21 22

23 24 25 26

Silent letters

WRITING: SPELLING

Unscramble the letters to make the silent **k** words in the box.

❶ **wekn** ❷ **kbon** ❸ **evakn**

❹ **deank** ❺ **ghtnik** ❻ **efikn**

❼ **tnik** ❽ **wonk** ❾ **ckonk**

knit	**know**	**knob**
knife	**knight**	**knead**
knock	**knew**	**knave**

Complete each of these words by adding a silent **b** or a silent **g**.

⓫ **nat**

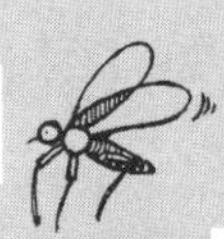

❿ **com**

⓬ **lim**

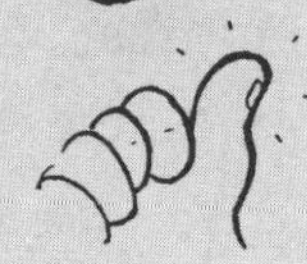

climb
comb **gnat**
gnaw **thumb**
gnome **limb**

⓰ **thum**

⓭ **nome**

⓯ **clim**

⓮ **naw**

---

ck When these letters appear at the end of a word we say only the **k** sound. Read the sentences and then complete the incomplete words. Use words from the box.

⓱ **The ship was a ______ck on the mighty ______ck.**

⓲ **The hen began to ______ck at Dad's ______ck.**

⓳ **She put the scarf round her ______ck and put the key in the ______ck.**

⓴ **He gave a huge ______ck and scored a goal.**

㉑ **This clock has a very loud ______ck.**

㉒ **Don't forget to ______ck at the door.**

deck	**peck**	**rock**	**chick**	**knock**	**chick**	**kick**
wreck	**neck**	**sock**	**lock**	**pick**	**lick**	**tick**

Reading carefully

READING

Read this extract from *Stellar News* very carefully.

> **PEACE IN OUR GALAXY** **Star date 2030**
>
> The eight members of the Peace Council met today and agreed at last to end all wars between neighbouring planets. Members voted unanimously for peace. Their decision was met with cheers from the crowds waiting outside the Council Hall.
>
> The President of the Council, Zelda the Just, said, "At last we can all live and work together in a new spirit of helpfulness and trust."

HOWEVER... she later received a note which said that the Council had traitors in its midst! Two hostile members were secretly plotting to overthrow the peace plans and take over the galaxy.

You can unmask the traitors! Read each of these descriptions, and match it to a picture. Write F (friend) or T (traitor) under each picture.

long hair straight hair spotted skin 2 small eyes 2 arms suckers for fingers 2 legs high collar F	long hair curly hair plain skin 3 small eyes 2 arms 5 fingers on each hand 2 legs neckband F	short hair straight hair scaly skin 1 large eye 2 arms 5 fingers on each hand 2 legs helmet F	short hair curly hair plain skin 1 small eye 2 arms claws for fingers 4 legs high collar F
long hair straight hair plain skin 2 large eyes 3 arms 3 fingers on each hand 3 legs helmet T	long hair curly hair plain skin 2 large eyes 2 arms claws for fingers 4 legs hat F	short hair straight hair spotted skin 2 eyes on stalks 2 arms claws for fingers 2 legs neckband T	short hair curly hair spotted skin 3 eyes on stalks 3 arms 3 fingers on each hand 3 legs hat F

These are the pictures from *Stellar News*.

Now that the traitors have been unmasked, what should Zelda do?
Discuss your ideas with an adult.

Letter strings

WRITING: SPELLING AND HANDWRITING

All the words in each of these two boxes end with the same letter string. Write the letter string, and then the complete word, in your joined style. Remember how it feels to write the letter string, and this will help you to remember the spelling.

1	si ght	sight
2	li	
3	ni	
4	kni	
5	fri	
6	hei	
7	mi	
8	wei	
9	ti	
10	ri	

11	look ing	looking
12	do	
13	see	
14	eat	
15	r	
16	fl	
17	sing	
18	act	
19	drink	
20	talk	

Solve these clues. All the answers end in the same letter string.

21 **Young cattle** cal

22 **More than one wife** wi

23 **Two of these make a whole.** hal

24 **Bread is shaped into these.** loa

Unscramble these words. They all end in **tch**.

25	tchwa	watch
26	idtch	
27	tchla	
28	sctchra	
29	tchac	
30	mtcha	

These words all end in **tion**, but they have been written back to front.
Turn them round, and then copy them in your joined style. Practise **tion** first.

tion **tion**

31 **noitats** s

32 **noitnevni**

33 **noitisop**

34 **noitcetorp**

35 **noitom**

Break the code to complete these words. They all end in **ough**.

a	b	c	d	e	f	g	h	i	j	k	l	m	n	o	p	q	r	s	t	u	v	w	x	y	z
22	23	24	25	26	1	2	3	4	5	6	7	8	9	10	11	12	13	14	15	16	17	18	19	20	21

36 13 **ough** → **rough**

37 24 **ough** →

38 15 3 **ough** →

39 15 3 13 **ough** →

40 26 9 **ough** →

41 15 13 **ough** →

42 11 7 **ough** →

43 15 **ough** →

Add **ed** to each of these words.

44 **happen** → **happened**

45 **listen** →

46 **call** →

47 **cook** →

48 **pick** →

Word fingers

WRITING: SPELLING

Look → Copy → Cover → Write → Check

Use this formula to help you to learn the spellings of these words.
Learn a 'handful' a day, and ask an adult to test you.

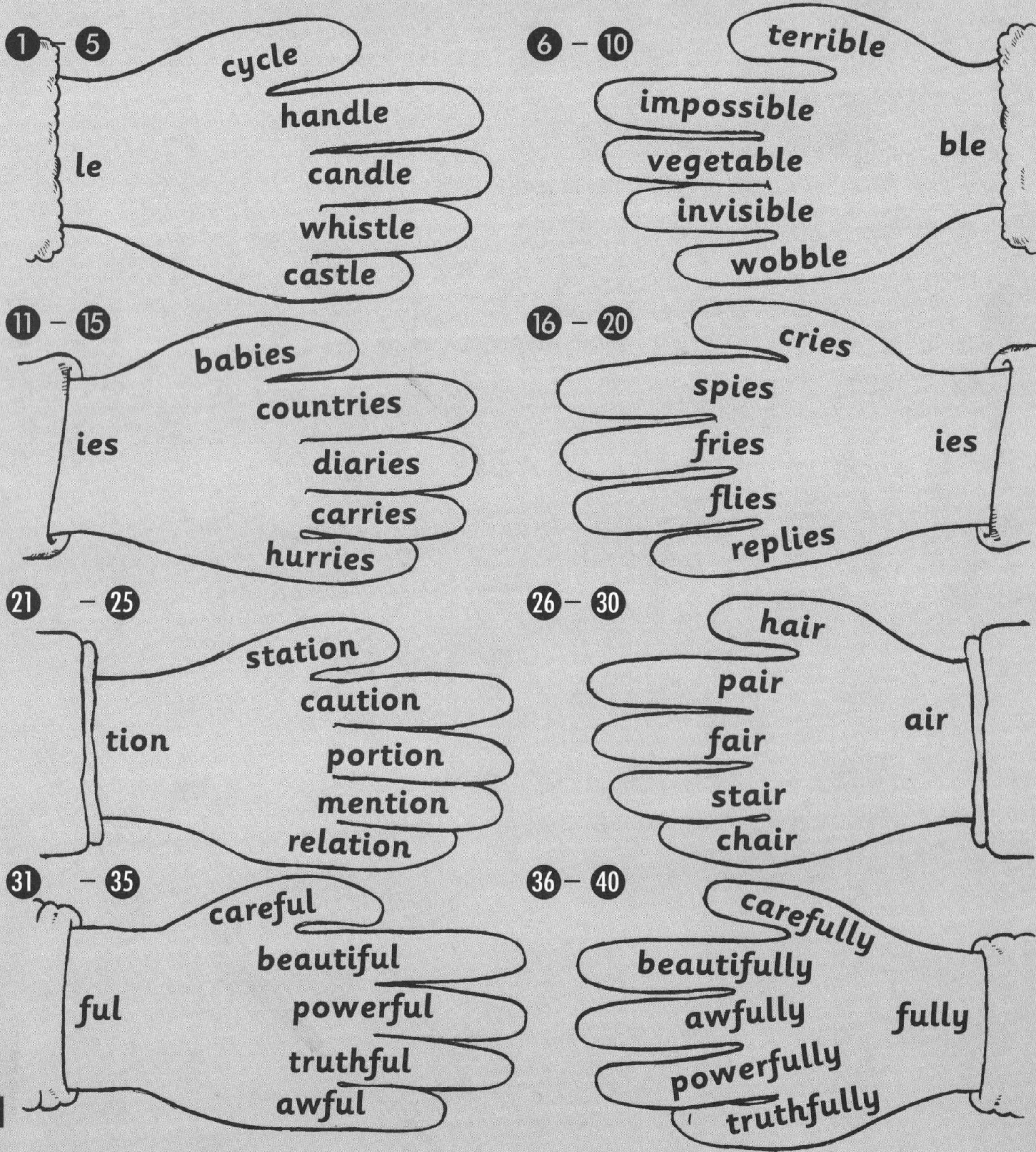

TEST 1

READING: COMPREHENSION (FICTION)

This passage is from a story called *The Jenius* by Dick King-Smith. Judy has had her guinea-pigs, Molly and Joe, for two years. Molly has begun to get a little podgy...

Read the passage carefully, skipping over the spaces, to get a sense of what it is about. Then read it again slowly to decide which words to put in the spaces. Finally, add the missing words, taking care to spell them correctly. (In some cases there is only one correct word, but in others, several words may be equally appropriate.)

But next morning, when she went to feed the ________-pigs, the white one, she found, looked quite different.

"Molly!" said Judy. "You look awfully thin. Whatever's ________ matter with you?"

This time they both answered, Molly with a series of small, happy squeaks, ________ Joe with a low, proud grumble, as they moved aside to ________ what had happened. There between them ________ a single, very large, baby guinea-pig, the child of their old age. It was partly white and smooth ________ its mother and partly red and rough like its ________.

To Judy's delight it stumbled forward on feet that seemed three sizes too ________, until it bumped the wire of the hutch-front ________ its huge head. Its eyes were very bright and seemed to shine with intelligence. Then it ________ a single word in guinea-pig language. Anyone could have told it meant "Hullo!"

"Oh!" said Judy. "Aren't ________ beautiful!"

"He gets it from his mother," chattered ________ in the background.

"And aren't you brainy!"

"He takes after his dad," ________ Molly.

Judy stared into the baby's eyes.

"You," she said, "are ________ to be the best-trained, most brilliant guinea-pig in the ________ world. And you're going to start lessons right ________. Now then. Sit!"

Of course, when you're only a few hours old, standing ________ be tiring, but was that the reason why Joe and Molly's son immediately ________ down?

SCORE

/ 18

Jumbled sentences

READING: COMPREHENSION (NON-FICTION)

Robin Hood lived in England in the Middle Ages, when King Richard I was fighting the Crusades. His brother Prince John looked after the country while he was away. The following sentences describe what happened, but each sentence has been jumbled. Write the sentences correctly in the spaces. Remember to put in the capital letters, commas and full stops.

1. **Prince made John pay people taxes very heavy the**
2. **many poor not pay outlaws could became people and**
3. **Robin one nobleman led of a band Sherwood Forest in called outlaws Hood**
4. **the Robin and outlaws his loved people poor the Men Merry**
5. **they rich John Prince gave poor to the money stole from and the**
6. **Merry Men hunted were the by Nottingham Robin and Sheriff his of**
7. **peace there was King Richard home came when at last**

What happened next?

WRITING: STORY WRITING

Who took the brooch?

Katie stared at the collection of Roman coins and jewellery that Miss Jones had borrowed from the local museum. The others stared too. Yes, there was definitely a space where the biggest brooch had been. With a cold feeling in her stomach, Katie remembered watching the new girl, Joanne, holding it in the palm of her hand and admiring it.

Now they had all stopped work on their project, and Miss Jones' mouth was just a tight, thin line as her eyes moved slowly round the class. She looked so angry that even Katie felt guilty.

But who had taken the brooch? Could it really have been Joanne? She had only been at Wilcox Road Primary for two weeks, and no one knew her very well yet.

What they did know was that she was not afraid of Brad. Brad was the class bully, and he and his gang made life difficult for anyone who would let them – but that didn't include Joanne. She always stood up to Brad – even laughed at him sometimes. Brad didn't like this at all, and now he spent most of his time plotting how to get her into trouble.

Katie's thoughts were interrupted by Miss Jones' voice. "I want you all to empty your pencil cases on to your desks, and turn out your pockets. No one is going to leave the room until that brooch has been found ..."

- Did Miss Jones find the brooch in Joanne's pencil case?
- Had Brad planted the brooch in Joanne's pencil case?
- Did someone see Brad planting the brooch in Joanne's pencil case? Did he get into trouble?
- Your own idea...

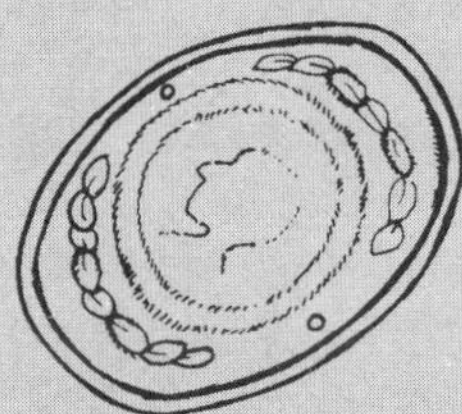

Make some notes about how the story might grow, and how it might end.

Writing a poem

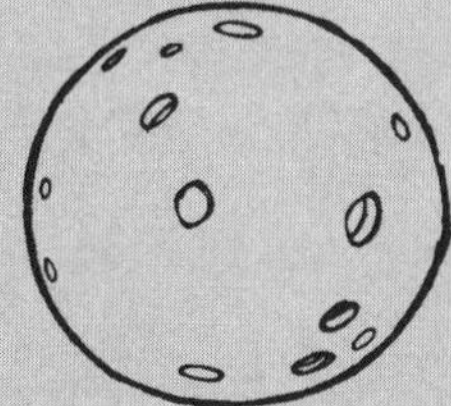

An intergalactic dash

Racing through the galaxy,
On a trip to Mars,
Shooting by an asteroid field,
Into a band of stars.

Skiing on the Milky Way,
There's Jupiter in sight!
Dodging past its mighty moons,
On our headlong flight.

We've fuel to last a light year,
And time enough to play,
I bet you've never guessed it –
It's a spaceman's holiday!

by Charlie Whiteford (age 11)

Copy the poem in your best joined handwriting. Use print (all capitals, or capitals and lower case letters) for the title. Try to write quickly but neatly. Try to keep each line in your head as you read it.

Punctuation marks

? A question mark is used instead of a full stop at the end of a sentence that asks a question.

! An exclamation mark is used instead of a full stop at the end of a sentence to show that the words have a special meaning. For example, it can be used to show anger, surprise, joy, danger or amusement. It can also be used to attract attention: **"Mum!"**

Put a question mark or an exclamation mark at the end of each of these sentences.

1. **I love going to the seaside** ☐
2. **Have you been on holiday** ☐
3. **Look out, it's going to fall** ☐
4. **Where is it** ☐
5. **What are you doing** ☐
6. **You can't do that** ☐
7. **Happy birthday, Gran** ☐
8. **How old are you** ☐

Speech marks are used to enclose the actual words that someone has spoken. The full stop changes to a comma:

My name is Lisa. ▲ **"My name is Lisa," she said.** ▲

Think of some actual words for these people to speak.
Write the words in the spaces.

9. " ______________________________ ," **growled the monster.**
10. " ______________________________ ," **said the teacher.**
11. " ______________________________ ," **whispered my friend.**
12. " ______________________________ ," **laughed the clown.**
13. " ______________________________ ," **said Auntie Cath kindly.**

What do you think these people are saying?
Write the actual words they speak,
and remember to include **,**, **!** or **?**.

Writing letters

Letters are written for many different purposes. You may want to write and complain about a television programme, or you may want to write fan mail to a pop star. You may have a penfriend, or a relative who needs cheering up.

Write a letter to a friend, telling him or her what preparations to make for a trip to an Outdoor Pursuits Adventure Camp. Pretend that you went last summer and that the friend is going next month (July). Keep to the purpose of the letter, and only give information that will be helpful to your friend.

Illustrate the borders of your letter. Don't forget to write your address.

Dear ________________

TEST 2

WRITING: HANDWRITING

Write an amusing letter to one of these people:

- a friend who is in hospital with a broken leg after an accident on his or her rollerblades
- a friend who has just moved to a safari centre in the African bush
- a relative who thinks you are wonderful (for example, Gran, Grandad, Auntie, a big brother/sister at college)

PLANNING SHEET

Name of friend/relative

Jokes he or she would like

Plans for a visit to, or from, him or her

Dear

SCORE

10

Capital letters and full stops

WRITING: GRAMMAR AND PUNCTUATION

A capital letter is needed at the start of a sentence, and a full stop is needed at the end. Read this passage carefully and then use a coloured pen to put in the capital letters and full stops.

It was as dark as the inside of your hat the wind was so loud that we couldn't hear each other speak at all we had to use hand signals all we needed now was for it to rain, and sure enough it did it came down in great bucketfuls we were soon soaked to the skin we both decided to wait for the school bus next time and not to walk home again

You do not need full stops after items in a list.

List your favourite toys/books/television programmes.

A list of my favourite ______________________

____

____

____

Abbreviations and contractions

WRITING: GRAMMAR AND PUNCTUATION

We use shortened versions of some words if we want to save space.

Units of measurement are abbreviated like this:

centimetre → cm

Find out the abbreviations for these.

1. **kilogram** ☐
2. **gram** ☐
3. **litre** ☐
4. **millilitre** ☐
5. **kilometre** ☐
6. **metre** ☐

Ordinal numbers (**first, second, third**) are abbreviated like this:

first → 1st **second → 2nd**

The numeral is followed by the last two letters of the word.

Write the abbreviations for these.

7 **third** ☐ 8 **sixth** ☐ 9 **ninth** ☐

10 **fourth** ☐ 11 **seventh** ☐ 12 **tenth** ☐

13 **fifth** ☐ 14 **eighth** ☐

People's titles (**Doctor, Mister**) and some place names are shortened like this:

Doctor → Dr. **Road → Rd.**

The first and last letters of the word are used, with a full stop at the end. This kind of abbreviation is called a contraction.

Write these contractions out in full.

15 **Mr.** ☐ 16 **Ave.** ☐

17 **St. (place)** ☐ 18 **St. (person)** ☐

19 **Revd.** ☐

Someone's "initials" are the first letter of their first name(s) followed by the first letter of their surname . Each letter is followed by a full stop:

Fred Smith → F. S.

Write the initials of these people.

20 **Ali Baker** ☐

21 **Sue Walker** ☐

22 **Tom Smith** ☐

23 **Ann White** ☐

Now write the initials of six members of your family or six friends.

24 ☐ 25 ☐

26 ☐ 27 ☐

28 ☐ 29 ☐

TEST 3

READING: COMPREHENSION (FICTION)

This passage is from a book called *A Gift from Winklesea* by Helen Cresswell.

This is the story of the gift, a beautiful stone, which Dan and Mary have bought for their mother. One day, in its place on the mantelpiece, it begins to grow warm and to hatch...

Dan and Mary shook their heads silently without moving their eyes from the jogging stone.

"The chips are getting cold," moaned Mrs. Kane. "Oh, dear, what a thing to happen!"

"Well, then," said Mr. Kane loudly, as if hoping that the egg would hear him, "we'll get on with our chips. We can't stand around all night looking at this thing showing off. Come along, Dan, come on, Mary, get on with your suppers. Take no notice of it."

They went slowly back to the table. They picked up their knives and forks again. All the while, louder and louder, came that tap, tapping as the egg jumped and jogged.

"Looks like being a nice day again tomorrow," said Mr. Kane loudly. "Though we could do with a drop of rain, for the lettuce and tomatoes."

Tap, tap, tap.

"The sweet peas look like doing nicely this year," almost shouted Mr. Kane.

At that moment the egg, with a final acrobatic leap, jumped right clear of the pedestal and landed smack at the feet of the glass cat. Mary and Mrs. Kane screamed together. Then, knives and forks poised in mid-air, they saw that the egg was split right across. Slowly the gap between the two halves widened. They stared.

"Do something," moaned Mrs. Kane again. "Quick, Alfred, do something."

"Shush!" said Mr. Kane. "Watch!"

And as they watched, a most perfectly beautiful neat, grey little creature parted the stone shell and stepped right out on to the polished tiles of the mantelpiece.

"It's a – it's a – what is it?" whispered Mrs. Kane.

"It's a baby kangaroo!" said Mary.

It quite obviously was not, but as nobody else had the least idea what it was, nobody bothered to contradict her. Outside a factory siren began to hoot and they all

jumped. Dan got up and went over to the mantelpiece.

"Dan!" cried Mrs. Kane. "Come away this minute!"

"It's all right, Mum," he said, "it won't bite. Look, you've frightened it now."

The Gift from Winklesea had gone behind the clock. It moved so swiftly that they hardly saw it go.

"Look at that!" exclaimed Mr. Kane admiringly. "Proper little greyhound!"

He too got up and went over. A small grey head and beady eye peered from behind the clock face.

"It's looking at us!" cried Mary. "Isn't it sweet!"

"I don't know about sweet," said Mrs. Kane. But she, too, came over and joined them. For a few minutes they all stood and looked at the Gift from Winklesea and the Gift from Winklesea looked back at them with a black, unblinking eye.

"Well, then," said Mr. Kane. "What's to be done now?"

"Perhaps it's hungry?" suggested Mary.

"That's it," agreed Mr. Kane, grateful for the idea. "Give it a chip, Dan."

Dan fetched one and laid it gently on the shelf a few inches away from the tiny creature. Gradually it came from behind the clock and edged forward.

"It's sniffing!" cried Mary.

It was. Then a mouth of astonishing size suddenly opened and as rapidly closed. The chip had gone.

"Well, bless me!" said Mrs. Kane.

Dan fetched another chip. Then another. Then another. The mouth opened and shut like clockwork.

"No more!" cried Mrs. Kane then. "You'll give the poor thing indigestion! It's only a baby, poor thing. Whatever next! Just out of its shell and you feeding it chips as if it was a navvy or something. Give it a saucer of milk, Mary, that's more like what it wants."

A saucer full of milk disappeared in one long, noisy suck.

"There!" cried Mrs. Kane triumphantly. "I knew it! Bless its little heart! It was milk he wanted, wasn't it, my lamb?"

The Gift from Winklesea gazed up at her with its black unwinking eyes.

"Now what?" said Mr. Kane. The meal seemed to be over.

"Where are we going to put it?" asked Dan.

They all thought.

"There's a mouse cage up in the loft," said Mary.

"No," said Mr. Kane. "The aquarium. That's what it wants – a bit of water."

"But you might drown it!" cried Mary.

"No harm in trying," he said. "It came out of the sea, didn't it? You fetch the tank, Dan, from out that cupboard under the sink. Put a bit of water in it and a stone or two, and we'll see what happens."

Half an hour later the Gift from Winklesea was happily swimming in its new home, stopping now and then to gobble the chips that Dan held over the side for it on a fork. Mr. Kane was out in the garden digging for worms in case it fancied one of those. Mrs. Kane was putting out a note for the milkman to order an extra pint of milk, and Mary just sat and watched, perfectly rapt. The Gift from Winklesea was one of the family now.

The story

1. What were the Kane family doing as they watched the egg?

2. What did the egg do after its "final acrobatic leap"?

3. What came out of the stone shell?

4. How did the Gift move?

   slowly ☐ clumsily ☐ swiftly ☐

5. What did they give it to eat?

   chips and milk ☐ fish and pop ☐ carrots and grass ☐

6. What was the reason Mr. Kane gave for thinking that an aquarium would be a good place to put the Gift?

The characters

7. Who was trying to ignore the egg just before it hatched?

8. The Gift seemed confident and at ease as the passage ended. Give two reasons.

9. How do you think Mrs. Kane knew what the Gift wanted?

The style

10. Tick the word(s) that you think describe the way in which this story is written.

seriously ☐ amusingly ☐ spookily ☐ excitingly ☐

11. Three things happen to the Gift in this passage. What are they?

12. Tick the statements which are true.

a This passage is action-packed. ☐

b There is a lot of conversation in it. ☐

c The Gift is described carefully. ☐

Your opinion

13. Did you enjoy reading this passage? Give reasons.

14. How would you feel if something like this happened in your home?

SCORE ___ / 14

Direct and indirect speech

WRITING: GRAMMAR AND PUNCTUATION

Speech which is enclosed in speech marks is called direct speech.
The punctuation mark goes inside the speech marks too:

"If I'm late I'll be furious!" said Tim.

Complete each speech with **,**, **?** or **!**.

1. **"What time is it   " asked Ann.**
2. **"I'm starving   " wailed Laura.**
3. **"Won't someone help   " gasped the man.**
4. **"Mum gave me a new book today   " said Jeni.**
5. **"My football club meets on Monday   " replied Jamie.**

We can also write speech like this:

Tim said that he would be furious if he was late.

We are reporting what Tim said, and not using his exact words.
Indirect speech does not use speech marks.
Change this indirect speech into direct speech.

6. **John said that he was going to be late.**

7. **Mr. Casey inquired when the next flight was due.**

8. **Samantha muttered that she was sorry.**

9. **Les asked how I was.**

10. **Pancho moaned that he felt very ill.**

A verb is a doing word. Some verbs describe ways of speaking:

"Well, hello!" <u>boomed</u> Mr. Stott.
"This is great!" <u>laughed</u> Tom.
"What can it be?" <u>whispered</u> Lucy.

Complete each of these with a suitable verb.

11 **"Oh, I am tired,"** ______ **Gran.**

12 **"Well, I'm full of beans!"** ______ **Sally.**

13 **"What is that?"** ______ **Sophie.**

14 **"Help! It's coming towards us!"** ______ **Kevin.**

TEST 4

WRITING: GRAMMAR AND PUNCTUATION

' An apostrophe can be used to show that something belongs to someone. If there is only one owner, we add **'s**:

The bag belonging to Andy → Andy<u>'s</u> bag

Now rewrite these, following the example above.

1 **the ball belonging to Sue**

2 **the food Pat was eating**

3 **the house where Leon lives**

4 **the book for the teacher**

5 **the hat Mum wears**

6 **the field for the pony**

7 **the car Dad owns**

8 **the milk for the cat**

9 **the scarf belonging to Al**

10 **the bone for Rover**

SCORE

/10

Writing stories

WRITING: STORY WRITING

Story writing is sometimes the hardest kind of writing because we have to think of ideas which will entertain a reader, and then develop them.

Stories have to be planned. A strong plot needs a beginning, a middle and an ending. The beginning sets the scene with an opening event and introduces the characters. The middle contains one or more main events, and the ending draws the events to a conclusion. You also need to think about the setting (where the story takes place), the characters, the time and the weather. Style is important too. This is the way in which you write to give your story a special atmosphere.

This is a storyboard. Storyboards are used for planning stories, and on this one you can see some ideas for different stories listed under the headings. Add two of your own ideas to each list.

Titles *Arctic Horror, Alien Head, A Friend for Life*

Settings	**Style**
a zoo, the Arctic, a tropical jungle, a school playground,	*amusing, mysterious, adventurous,*
Characters	**Times**
four friends aged 9, two dogs, a bank robber, a computer,	*midnight, winter, one hot afternoon, Christmas,*

Weather
snowy, a sandstorm, a blistering hot day, a frosty day,

Opening events
an Arctic explorer sets off on a dangerous expedition, a 9 year-old girl sees strange lights in the sky, a dog is abandoned in the middle of a city,

Main events
a dog is rescued from an old mine and treasure is found, a wicked teacher is caught stealing the school fund, an alien beams the class up to a spaceship,

Endings
a brave act solves all the problems, a dog finds a good home at last with a lonely person, the class learn to be kind to others after their space adventure,

Now think of five interesting or exciting beginnings and endings.

Beginnings	Endings
One dark, misty night...	...and nobody ever found out where the exploding trainers had been hidden.

Think about a story **you** have read and enjoyed.
Make notes about it on this storyboard.

STORYBOARD **Title**	
Setting	**Style**
Characters	**Time** **Weather**
Opening event	
Main events	
Ending	

TEST 5

WRITING: STORY WRITING

Choose one of the titles below and plan a short story. It should be lively and interesting, with plenty of ideas to keep the reader's attention. The plan should take you about 15 minutes.

The biggest night of my life

The 5,000 year-old man

Title (2 points)	
Setting (2 points)	**Style** (2 points)
Characters (2 points)	**Time** (1 point)
	Weather (1 point)
Opening event (3 points)	
Main events (4 points)	
Ending (3 points)	

SCORE

20

TEST 6

WRITING: STORY WRITING

Look at the story plan you wrote in Test 5.
Now write your story here. It should take about 30 minutes.
Try to fit the story into this space.

SCORE

/25

Verb tenses

Verbs (doing words) can be used to show differences in time:

He sang a song. (past tense)
He sings beautifully. (present tense)
He will sing later. (future tense)

Sort these verbs into tenses.

	past	present	future
1	saw	sees	will see
2			
3			
4			
5			

Underline the verb in each of these sentences. Use red for the past tense, blue for the present tense and green for the future tense.

6. I went to my Gran's house.
7. I will be going to the cinema tonight.
8. My mum is riding her horse.
9. Natasha sings beautifully.
10. I will write to my friend today.
11. I ate all my dinner.

Animal crossword

WRITING: SPELLING

CLUES

Across

This animal...

3 is the largest of the apes
5 says "oom" backwards
6 is a reddish-brown ape from Borneo
8 is an African or Indian giant
9 has powerful "jaws"
11 wears a dinner jacket in the Antarctic

Down

This animal...

1 has its own bag for carrying fish
2 may wear shoes
3 sounds rich, and swims
4 is the star of a cartoon set in Africa
7 has horns, and runs very fast
10 is Australia's best highjumper (a nickname)

Answers

Page 2 Hidden words

1–10 oil point soil foil boil (red)
royal oyster boy annoy joy (green)

11 point **12** royal
13 foil **14** boy
15 boil **16** oyster
17 enjoy **18** soil

19 boil **20** boy
21 enjoy **22** foil
23 oyster **24** point
25 royal **26** soil

Page 3 – Silent letters

1 knew **2** knob
3 knave **4** knead
5 knight **6** knife
7 knit **8** know
9 knock

10 comb **11** gnat
12 limb **13** gnome
14 gnaw **15** climb
16 thumb

17 wreck rock
18 peck sock
19 neck lock
20 kick **21** tick
22 knock

Pages 4–5 Reading carefully

Frank and Jim are the traitors (T).

Pages 6–7 Letter strings

1 ght sight **2** ght light
3 ght night **4** ght knight
5 ght fright **6** ght height
7 ght might **8** ght weight
9 ght tight **10** ght right

11 ing looking **12** ing doing
13 ing seeing **14** ing eating
15 ing ring **16** ing fling
17 ing singing **18** ing acting
19 ing drinking
20 ing talking

21 calves **22** wives
23 halves **24** loaves

25 watch **26** ditch
27 latch **28** scratch
29 catch **30** match

31 station **32** invention
33 position **34** protection
35 motion

36 rough **37** cough
38 though **39** through
40 enough **41** trough
42 plough **43** tough

44 happened **45** listened
46 called **47** cooked
48 picked

Page 8 – Word fingers

1–40 Help your child to remember the formula 'Look, copy, cover, write, check'.

Page 9 TEST 1

guinea the and show was like father big with spoke you Joe squeaked going whole away can sat

Alternative answers are acceptable if they make sense.

Page 10 – Jumbled sentences

1 Prince John made the people pay very heavy taxes.

2 Many poor people could not pay and became outlaws.

3 One nobleman, called Robin Hood, led a band of outlaws in Sherwood Forest.

4 The poor people loved Robin and his outlaws, the Merry Men.

5 They stole from rich Prince John and gave the money to the poor.

6 Robin and his Merry Men were hunted by the Sheriff of Nottingham.

7 When King Richard came home there was peace at last.

Page 11 – What happened next?

Check for careful reading and discuss possible endings. The child should then be able to make notes about one possible outcome.

Pages 12–13 Writing a poem

Encourage neat, even presentation.

Pages 14–15 Punctuation marks

1 ! **2** ?
3 ! **4** ?
5 ? **6** !
7 ! **8** ?

9–13 Accept any appropriate speeches.

14–18 Make sure speech marks, commas, exclamation marks and question marks have been used correctly.

Page 16 Writing letters

Encourage your child to keep to the subject, and to write in clear sentences with correct punctuation.

Page 17 TEST 2

Award 1 point for each planning idea. Award 7 points for the letter:
1 for prose style
1 for punctuation
1 for neatness
1 for inclusion of planned items
1 for concentration
1 for keeping to the subject
1 for originality

Page 18 Capital letters and full stops

Check that capital letters have been included/omitted appropriately.

Pages 18–19 Abbreviations and contractions

1 kg **2** g
3 l **4** ml
5 km **6** m

7 3rd **8** 6th
9 9th **10** 4th
11 7th **12** 10th
13 5th **14** 8th

15 Mister **16** Avenue
17 Street **18** Saint
19 Reverend

20 A.B. **21** S.W.
22 T.S. **23** A.W.

24–29 Make sure the initials are correct, and followed by full stops.

Pages 20–23 TEST 3

1 They were having their tea.

2 It jumped off of the pedestal and landed at the feet of the glass cat.

3 a most perfectly beautiful neat, grey little creature

4 swiftly

5 chips and milk

6 He thought it needed water because it came from the sea.

7 Mr. Kane

8 It had food and a place to live.

9 Mrs. Kane knew that a baby animal needs milk because she had babies herself.

10 amusingly

11 It hatches, it eats and drinks, and it finds a home.

12 a✔ b✔

13–14 Award a point for a thoughtful answer expressed in correct English.

Pages 24–25 Direct and indirect speech

1 "What time is it?" asked Ann.

2 "I'm starving!" wailed Laura.

3 "Won't someone help?" gasped the man.

4 "Mum gave me a new book today," said Jeni.

5 "My football club meets on Monday," replied Jamie.

6 "I am going to be late," said John.

7 "When is the next flight due?" inquired Mr. Casey.

8 "I'm sorry," muttered Samantha.

9 "How are you?" asked Les.

10 ""I feel very ill!" moaned Pancho.

11–14 Accept all suitable verbs.

Page 25 TEST 4

1 Sue's ball
2 Pat's food
3 Leon's house
4 the teacher's book
5 Mum's hat
6 the pony's field
7 Dad's car
8 the cat's milk
9 Al's scarf
10 Rover's bone

Pages 26–27 Writing stories

Discuss the features of a story with your child. In the last exercise, you may need to help your child to analyse the chosen story.

Page 28 TEST 5

Award points as shown on the page. Take into account the originality of the ideas and the way they are put together.

Page 29 TEST 6

Award 25 points as follows:
10 for following the plan
3 for spelling
3 for grammar and punctuation
3 for handwriting
6 for originality and style

Page 30 Verb tenses

1 saw sees will see
2 rode is riding will ride
3 ran runs will run
4 sat sits will sit
5 looked is looking will look

6 went (red)
7 will be going (green)
8 is riding (blue)
9 sings (blue)
10 will write (green)
11 ate (red)

Page 31 Animal crossword

Across
(3) gorilla (5) cow
(6) orangutan (8) elephant
(9) shark (11) penguin

Down
(1) pelican (2) horse
(3) goldfish (4) lion
(7) antelope (10) roo

The African Grasslands

Alan Trussell-Cullen

Nelson Thornes

Nelson Thornes

First published in 2007 by Cengage Learning Australia
www.cengage.com.au

This edition published in 2008 under the imprint of Nelson Thornes Ltd,
Delta Place, 27 Bath Road, Cheltenham, United Kingdom, GL53 7TH

10 9 8 7 6 5 4 3 2
11 10 09 08

The African Grasslands
ISBN 978-1-4085-0131-3

Text by Alan Trussell-Cullen
Edited by Johanna Rohan
Designed by Vonda Pestana
Series Design by James Lowe
Production Controller Seona Galbally
Photo Research by Gillian Cardinal
Audio recordings by Juliet Hill, Picture Start
Spoken by Matthew King and Abbe Holmes
Printed in China by 1010 Printing International Ltd

Website www.nelsonthornes.com

Acknowledgements
The author and publisher would like to acknowledge permission to reproduce material from the following sources:
Photographs by Age fotostock/Werner Bollmann, p. 8 top/ John Glover, p. 23 right; Auscape International/ Ferrero Labat, pp. 4-5 /B.S.I.P., p. 23 top; Getty Images/Beverly Joubert, front cover centre/ Photodisc/Tom Brakefield, pp. 12-13 top/ Wolhuter Media, pp. 12-13 bottom/ Kim Wolhuter, p. 20/ J. Sneesby/B. Wilkins, p. 21/ Eastcott Momatiuk; Istockphoto, back cover right, pp. 4, 5; Istockphoto/Julie Maree, front cover right/ Jeremy Edwards, p. 7/ Pauline Wilson, p. 10/ Norma Reid, p. 11/ Andy Green, p. 17 bottom/ Derek Demmann, back cover, p. 18 bottom; Photolibrary/Mark Deeble & Victoria Stone, p. 6/ Hilary Pooley, p. 8 bottom/ Robert Francis, pp. 3, 9/ Mark Boulton, p. 14/ David Paynter, p. 15/ ifa-Bilderteam Gmbh, p. 16/ John Downer, pp. 17 top, 19 bottom/ Paul Goldstein, pp. 18-19 top.

The African Grasslands

Alan Trussell-Cullen

Contents

Chapter 1	**The African Grasslands' Food Chain**	4
Chapter 2	**Plants**	6
Chapter 3	**Plant-Eating Animals**	10
Chapter 4	**Predators**	16
Chapter 5	**Decomposers**	22
Glossary and Index		24

Chapter 1

THE AFRICAN GRASSLANDS' FOOD CHAIN

The African grasslands are close to the **equator**, where it's hot all year.
It rains there for part of the year, and for the rest of the year it's very hot and dry.

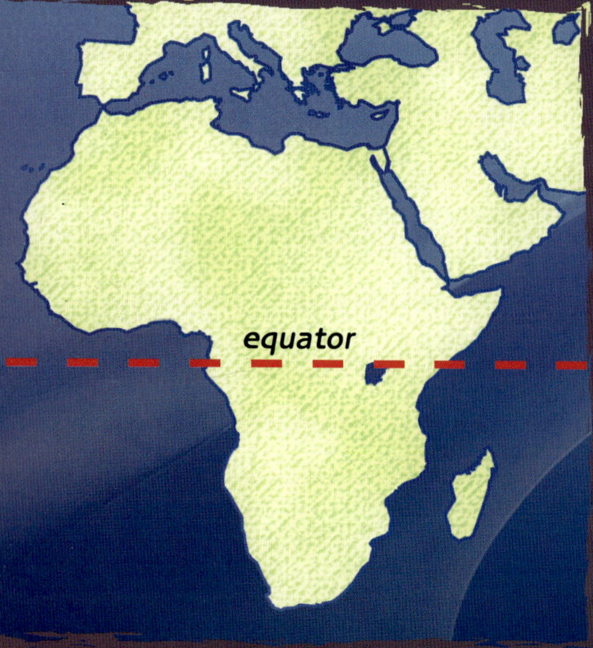

Many kinds of plants and animals live in the African grasslands.

Food links all living things in this **habitat**, and together all these links make up a food chain.

Chapter 2

PLANTS

Plants are the first link in the food chain. Plants are the only living things that can make their own food.

Plants make food from water and **carbon dioxide** using **chlorophyll** in their leaves and energy from the sun.

Plants are called **producers** because they produce food.

Grass is an important producer
in the African grasslands' food chain.
It grows quickly when it's wet
and survives most of the year
when it's very hot and dry.

In the African grasslands,
there is not enough rain throughout the year
for forests to grow.
But, some trees and bushes can survive.

baobab trees

Most of the trees in the African grasslands are acacias.
They often look flat on top.
Giraffes eat the leaves from below.

Baobab trees also grow in the African grasslands.
They can store lots of water in the soft wood of their trunks.

Chapter 3

PLANT-EATING ANIMALS

Animals need food for energy, but they can't make their own food. Animals get their food from plants or from other animals that eat plants. Animals are called **consumers**.

Plant-eating animals, like elephants, are the second link in the food chain. They are called primary consumers.

Zebras and wildebeest are also primary consumers. They can often be seen in the African grasslands eating grass near each other.

The grass in the African grasslands
goes brown and stops growing
in the driest part of the year.

When this happens,
animals go to look for food in other places.

Each year up to 1.5 million wildebeest set out
on a long journey to find food.
They return when the rains come again.

Many plant-eating animals
have body parts that help them get food.
The giraffe uses its long neck to reach
the high leaves of the acacia trees.
Other animals can't reach this high.

Elephants are huge animals,
and need lots of food.
They have long trunks
that are good for
reaching and grabbing food.
They also have teeth and strong jaws
that are good for crushing plants.
They eat grass, flowers, leaves, and bark.

Chapter 4

PREDATORS

Predators are the third link in the food chain. They are called secondary consumers because they get their food from eating other animals.

a leopard

a lion

Leopards, hyenas and lions are predators in the African grasslands' food chain.

a hyena

Lions live in groups called prides.

There can be up to 25 lions in a pride.

It's usually the job of the female lions in the pride to hunt.

Females hunt in groups at night.

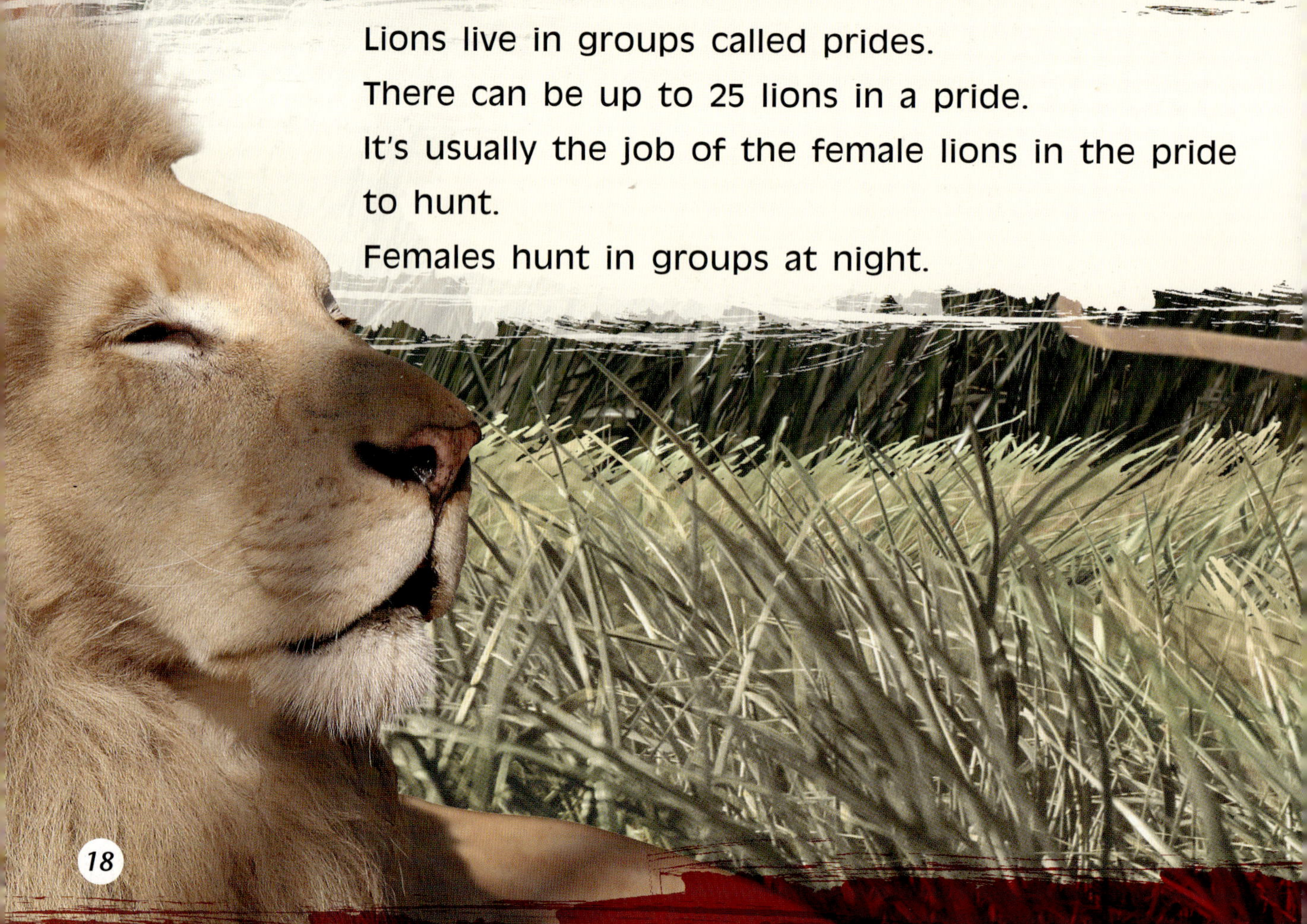

Lions prey on animals that aren't as fast as them, like wildebeest, zebras and antelopes. They have pointed teeth to grip and tear their **prey**.

Leopards hunt at night, like lions.
They prey on the same animals as lions,
and also on reptiles and birds.

Hyenas prey on wildebeest and zebras, but they are **scavengers**.
This means they eat the remains of other predators' prey.
Hyenas have powerful jaws and sharp teeth that help them eat bone and tough skin.

Chapter 5

DECOMPOSERS

Decomposers are the final link
in the African grasslands' food chain.

Decomposers such as bacteria, fungi and worms
help to break down dead plant
and animal material.
This material goes back into the soil
to help plants grow.

bacteria
earthworms

Glossary

carbon dioxide	a colourless, odourless gas
chlorophyll	a green pigment found in plants that helps them absorb energy from the Sun
consumers	animals that consume plants and other animals for food energy
decomposers	bacteria, fungi and worms that break down dead plant and animal materials
equator	an imaginary line on the Earth dividing it into the northern and southern hemispheres
habitat	the natural home or environment of an animal
predators	animals that eat other animals
producers	things that make something
prey	animals eaten by predators
scavengers	animals that eat dead animals

Index

acacias 9, 14
antelopes 19

baobab trees 9

carbon dioxide 6
chlorophyll 6

elephants 15
equator 4

giraffe 9, 14
grass 7, 12, 15

hyena 17, 21

leopard 16, 17, 20
lion 17, 18, 19, 20

wildebeest 11, 13, 19

zebras 11, 19